ALDEBURGH REVISITED

A Portrait of a Seaside Town

Diana Hughes

THE ALDEBURGH MUSEUM
IN ASSOCIATION WITH
THE ALDEBURGH BOOKSHOP

ACKNOWLEDGEMENTS

I have to acknowledge my deep gratitude to the *Aldeburgh Diary* written by the late JP Bristow and now sadly out of print. It introduced me to the history of Aldeburgh many years ago and is still my constant companion.

Most of the images in this book come from the Aldeburgh Museum Photographic Archive but there were inevitably gaps and I want to thank the following for their kindness and generosity in supplying my needs: Suffolk County Council; Frederick Warne & Co. for permission to reproduce the cover of *Orlando the Marmalade Cat*; English Heritage (NMR); The Landmark Trust; The Britten-Pears Foundation; Tony Pick of Coastal Images; Chloe Fraser Steele; The Aldeburgh Yacht Club; The Aldeburgh and District Local History Society; Margaret Young and members of the Garrett family.

Susan Fleming has meticulously read the whole manuscript and thus taken a great weight off my mind.

A large debt is owed to the Trustees and volunteers of the Aldeburgh Museum for their interest and support. I particularly want to thank Bob Prince who set up the whole project and has always been on hand to offer advice and his photographic skills when needed.

The exciting illustration of the Moot Hall and market place was realised by Richard Bonson and is based upon original research and illustrations.

David Gillingwater and Dawn Suffling of Herring Bone Design have made this book a thing of beauty. I thank them for their enthusiasm and quite extraordinary patience.

Finally a very big thank you to the Aldeburgh Bookshop for their most generous sponsorship, without which the book would never have been published.

The Aldeburgh Bookshop,
42 High Street, Aldeburgh,
Suffolk. IP15 5AB
Tel/fax: 01728 452389
email: johnandmary@aldeburghbookshop.co.uk

Printed and bound in Great Britain by
Fuller Davies Ltd, Ipswich.

2 4 6 8 10 9 7 5 3 1

ISBN 978-0-9531004-5-3

For
Rosie and Louis
who love their history

PREFACE

Pay a visit to the Museum on the sea-front in Aldeburgh and you will come face to face with the history of the town. You will see how the fortunes of an unimportant little fishing village changed some time after 1500, when its shifting coast-line opened up a sheltered harbour, which soon became a thriving centre for ship-building and trade.

The Moot Hall, which houses the Museum, is a superb timber-framed building, erected by the Burgesses of Aldeburgh in about 1550 as a symbol of their new-found prosperity. Sited in the middle of the town it served as Town Hall and focus for the market. There were shops and a gaol downstairs, a splendid meeting room and office upstairs. The future looked rosy.

Two hundred years later and everything had changed. The sea had overwhelmed many homes, erosion had eaten into the coast-line and the Town Hall was now on the edge of the sea; the Haven was silting up and could no longer accommodate big ships. Poverty visited Aldeburgh; houses were deserted; people were hungry.

But then, just as it seemed that the town was doomed, holiday-makers discovered the town. First it was rich, aristocratic families, who disdained the bustling south-coast resorts and came to find tranquillity and elegant society in Aldeburgh. They built grand houses, promenaded beside the sea in all their finery, and began to dip their toes in the water. They were soon followed by more modest visitors and the fortunes of the town revived.

This is the story I have tried to tell. There is a wealth of information to be found in the Museum and a vast archive of wonderful old prints and photographs that I have ransacked to illustrate Aldeburgh's story. My project began as a series of display boards for use in the Museum and these have now been transformed into a book to interest a wider public. I hope the reader finds the story as fascinating and rewarding as I have and perhaps one or two may feel inspired to undertake a little research for themselves.

'ALDE BURH'

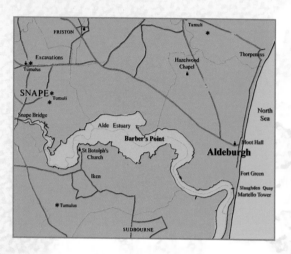

Alde burh is a Saxon name meaning *old defended enclosure.* This suggests that when the Saxons came they found the remains of an old – Roman – settlement at the mouth of the river and took over the site for themselves. There are no written records but archaeology supports this theory and it is now thought that in the second century there may have been a Roman port at the river mouth and another small Roman settlement three miles along the north bank of the river at Barber's Point.

The existence of a Saxon trading post now under the sea, seems highly probable; *Slaughting* (Slaughden) is a Saxon name.

BARBER'S POINT

Excavations at Barber's Point in 2004 and 2006 by the Aldeburgh & District Local History Society have uncovered both Romano-British pottery and evidence of a later Saxon settlement.

Oyster shells found in a Roman rubbish pit.

Digging at Barber's Point September 2004. On both sides of the river there is evidence of a Romano-British salt-working industry.

Excavated post hole, indicating the existence of a timber-framed building, probably Saxon.

Bricquetage: clay lining used in the extraction of salt from sea water.

Neolithic arrow head left behind by a much earlier visitor.

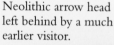

The rim of a clay amphora imported from Spain full of olive oil.

The top of a delicate Roman flagon found in 2006.

The head of the statue of the Roman Emperor Claudius probably thrown triumphantly into the River Alde after Boudicca sacked Roman Colchester in 60AD.

Roman pots found in the river with the remains of 'porridge' inside them. One is encrusted with barnacles.

SNAPE

At Snape Cross Roads the Anglo-Saxons used the site of a much earlier Bronze Age burial place for their cemetery.

Beneath one of the mounds at Snape was found the imprint of an Anglo-Saxon clinker-built boat, used perhaps for a royal burial. The grave, previously robbed, still contained a beautiful gold ring, set with a re-used Roman intaglio, and the fragments of a glass claw beaker.

Grave 46 fully excavated, showing a perfectly preserved body stain.

Complete cremation urn found containing quite a large amount of cremated bone.

© Suffolk County Council

Twill cloak or blanket covering a woman's burial.

THE PROSPEROUS YEARS

In the twelfth and thirteenth centuries the great port of Dunwich dominated the East Coast. Its excellent haven (harbour) sheltered many 'great ships' and fishing boats. Aldeburgh, with no haven, was an insignificant fishing village. But as storm followed storm the fortunes of Dunwich declined, while to the north of Aldeburgh a haven was opening up. By 1500 Aldeburgh was emerging as a port. Evidence of the town's growing prosperity can be found in the Chamberlains' Account Book and in two big building projects.

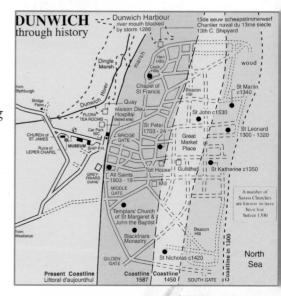

ALDEBURGH CHURCH

Before 1500 Aldeburgh Church consisted of just tower and nave. Now the North and South chapels were added and a little later these were extended to form aisles. 1524 saw the roof of the nave and the tower arch raised, then in 1545 the chancel was added. The Elizabethan church would have looked much as it does today, but the churchyard extended to the middle of the present road until 1824.

The Church was used for many secular purposes. Ship-auctions were regularly held in the nave. London theatre companies like this one toured the provinces and several came to Aldeburgh. It is possible that Shakespeare played in our Church.

MOOT HALL

In about 1550 a new, high-status building was erected in the centre of Aldeburgh to serve as Council Chamber, focus for the Market and prison – the Town Hall. (The name Moot Hall was bestowed upon it much later by the Victorians.)

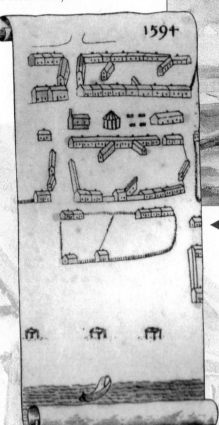

This fragment from an old map shows the Town Hall quite soon after it was built. The ground floor opened on to the market and was occupied by six self-contained shops and two prison cells. The round building with the pointed roof was the Market Cross, which would have been surrounded by stalls. Market days (Wednesdays and Saturdays) would have been lively affairs, very noisy and smelly. The market opened and closed to the ringing of the market bell. Hours: 9–3 in summer; 10–2 in winter. Trading outside these hours was not permitted.

Upstairs (there were only outside stairs) there was a large meeting room and a much smaller room at the southern end.

The Town Hall looking south c1760. The barrier across the road marked the limit of the market. There was another barrier to the north. The building to the east of the Market Cross is a mystery.

MARKET DAY IN ALDEBURGH C1590

An artist's realisation of the scene outside Aldeburgh Town Hall on a market day c1590. The houses stretching to the north and east come as a surprise, but there are documents and maps which prove they were there, although we can only guess at their appearance. There is a little guess-work too, about the appearance of the market stalls, but the Town Hall and its shops must have looked just like this.

THE BOROUGH

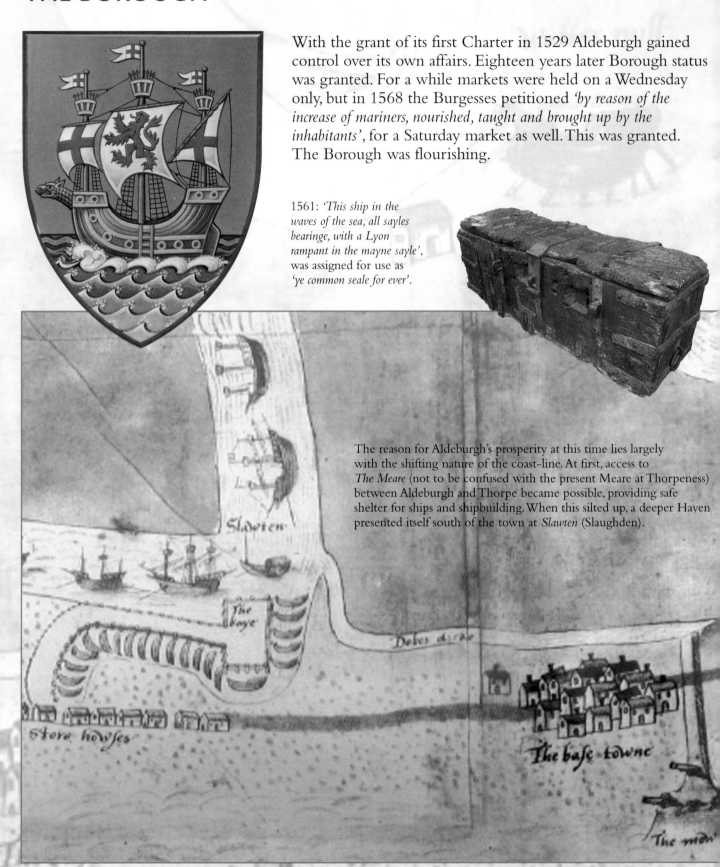

With the grant of its first Charter in 1529 Aldeburgh gained control over its own affairs. Eighteen years later Borough status was granted. For a while markets were held on a Wednesday only, but in 1568 the Burgesses petitioned *'by reason of the increase of mariners, nourished, taught and brought up by the inhabitants'*, for a Saturday market as well. This was granted. The Borough was flourishing.

1561: *'This ship in the waves of the sea, all sayles bearinge, with a Lyon rampant in the mayne sayle'*, was assigned for use as *'ye common seale for ever'*.

The reason for Aldeburgh's prosperity at this time lies largely with the shifting nature of the coast-line. At first, access to *The Meare* (not to be confused with the present Meare at Thorpeness) between Aldeburgh and Thorpe became possible, providing safe shelter for ships and shipbuilding. When this silted up, a deeper Haven presented itself south of the town at *Slawten* (Slaughden).

Slawten

The Haye

Dobes ditche

Store howses

The base towne

The midi

A NEW BOROUGH

The new Borough was governed by a group of leading citizens called Burgesses. There were twelve Capital or Superior Burgesses and twenty-four Inferior Burgesses. Every Sunday the Burgesses processed from the Moot Hall to the Church splendidly arrayed in their robes of office.

Aldeburgh won the right to return two MPs to Parliament in 1571. It continued to do so until the Reform Act of 1832. *Roger Woodhouse, Esq. and Robert Hihfourd, gent.* were the first members to be elected—by a very limited electorate.

This map from the time of Elizabeth I shows that many smaller boats were drawn up by capstans and berthed on the beach. Note the beacons on Firetree Hill—the Terrace today: they were used both to guide boats inshore and as a warning of danger. There were cannon on the beach—this was the time of the Armada threat—and a bulwark with five cannon called *The Mount* (Fort Green).

HOME AFFAIRS - 17th CENTURY

The early years of the seventeenth century saw many violent and destructive storms lash our shores: flimsy lathe and plaster cottages were damaged by wind and waves and many were lost to the sea.

Musician

Apprentice going to fetch water

Shipbuilding and trade were thriving. Fishermen had a hard time battling the weather, but catches were good. Herring and sprats were caught locally (there were many smoke-houses in the town) and every year the Icelandic fleet set out in search of cod and other deep-sea fish. Porpoises were regularly caught with the fish and were highly prized: they were often sent as presents or 'sweeteners' to friends and superiors by the Burgesses.

Some of the townsfolk must have been less than responsible about controlling their animals, because an Order was made by the Burgesses imposing strict penalties upon anyone who allowed his *'Swyne Cossett Lambes Shepe Gese or Duckes'* to roam the streets and cause damage and annoyance to others.

POOR RELIEF

Poverty was growing as the result of increasing demands for money and men for the Civil War; there were also outbreaks of sickness and attacks by pirates. But the town did its best to look after its orphans and poor children.

One boy the town cared for very well was 'Blind Harry'. He must have been a talented musician because considerable sums were spent buying him instruments. He was apprenticed to a musician—probably one of the town waits.

An Aldeburgh smoke house

1643 William Dowsing was sent into East Anglia by Parliament to eradicate any symbols of high church practice that had survived the Reformation. In his journal he wrote: '*Aldborough, Jan 24th. We gave order for taking down 20 Cherubims, and 38 Pictures, which their Lecturer Mr Swayn (a godly man) undertook and their Captain Mr Johnson.*' Captain Johnson, the most important man in Aldeburgh during the Civil War, and the godly Mr Swayne (a preacher) carried out Dowsing's instructions with enthusiasm and even exceeded them: many brasses were also removed or partially destroyed and carvings in the roof demolished.

WITCHES ARE HANGED & ALDEBURGH DECLINES

Matthew Hopkins, self-styled Witch Finder General, and widow Phillips, his *search woman,* were employed by the Burgesses to *find out* witches in Aldeburgh at a time of mass-hysteria against witches throughout East Anglia. Seven women were incarcerated behind this barred window in the Moot Hall's prison in the middle of winter. They were prevented from sleeping and *watched* for proof of their guilt – the coming of their *familiar spirits.* Eventually, cold, hungry and exhausted, they must have *confessed.*

The witches were hanged in town in February 1646. Hopkins was paid £2 for giving evidence against them, widow Phillips £1. John Paine who hanged them received 11s (55p) for his pains. William Daniell set up the gallows - £1, and Henry Lawrence provided the rope for seven halters and made the knots – 8s (40p). Beer was provided to keep up the spirits of the onlookers. Altogether the cost of ridding the town of these poor women was tremendous and a special rate had to be raised to meet it.

◄ The front page of Hopkins book illustrates the *familiars* thought to carry out a witch's devilish intentions. These creatures were supposed to suckle evil power from their witch. They were thought to be able to cause the sudden and violent illness (and sometimes the death) of those who thwarted the witch.

Hopkins died soon after the witches, probably of TB. He was only 26. ►

By 1650 Aldeburgh was in decline. Men and money were required to fight a series of trade wars against the Dutch while the Civil War made huge demands. (In 1643 Parliamentary soldiers were quartered in the Church.) Plague and smallpox caused many deaths. Fishermen lost their boats and their lives to marauding pirates.

Civil War soldier

POVERTY

In 1662 the Hearth Tax Return shows Aldeburgh with 77 houses occupied, 34 empty and 25 certificates of poverty. The many beggars and poor people had to be supported by a declining population. A population of over 1300 in 1603 had fallen to below 650 by 1670.

SOLE BAY. 1672.

The terrible and pointless Battle of Sole Bay, fought off Southwold in 1672, was claimed as a victory by both sides but in reality was inconclusive. Many sailors were cast on shore and upon the charity of the nearest town.

FIRST BATHING MACHINE & THE MARTELLO TOWER

A steady if unspectacular trade with London continued through the eighteenth century with mostly butter and grain going out and fancy goods such as wines, linens and tobacco coming in. And coals came from Newcastle. The end of Marlborough's wars, however, meant unemployment for a lot of seamen. Many of them took to smuggling on a large scale. If the coastguards could neither be bribed nor terrorised, the smugglers fought them. In 1727, they caught a conscientious officer near Snape and sliced off his nose.

▲ The High Street in 1790 as depicted on an old chart.

▼ The sea continued to take its toll and by 1790 a map shows the Town Hall with nothing between it and the waves. In the next few years the Market Cross would disappear.

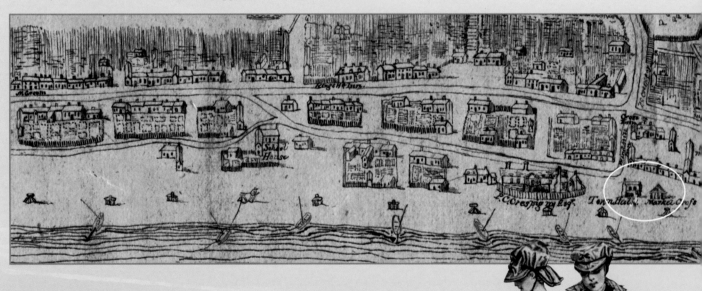

Alongside considerable poverty, sea-bathing began to be fashionable. In 1764 comes one of the first mentions of a bathing machine; '...*there is a curious machine that by the assistance of a single person may be run into the sea to any depth proper for bathing*'.

The Martello Tower was built between 1808 and 1812. It was the most northerly of a chain of 103 defensive towers built to withstand the threat of invasion by the French, led by the Emperor Napoleon. When built the towers were called heavy gun batteries and were designed for four guns. Only 43 remain today.

The Aldeburgh tower did not originally stand on its own as it does today. It was once part of the hamlet of Slaughden which finally vanished due to erosion in the early years of the twentieth century. It has the distinction of being the only Martello Tower to be quatrefoil in shape; all the other towers were round or oval.

© English Heritage (NMR)

By 1815 the invasion threat was over; Napoleon was defeated at Waterloo. The largest and most costly coastal defence system in English history never fired a shot in anger.

In 1936 the almost derelict tower was sold to Miss Debenham who had it restored, and built an *'elegant penthouse'* on its top. By 1971 the thirties penthouse had in turn become derelict and the tower itself was in decay. It was rescued by the Landmark Trust who restored it to provide comfortable holiday accommodation.

REGENCY RESORT

By 1800 Aldeburgh, *'impoverished and depopulated by the encroachment of the sea, was hastening to decay, but then the titled families, encouraged by the Hanoverian craze for the sea, began to recognise Aldeburgh and preferred it to the crowded beaches of the South Coast'*. Roads were improved and superior houses built, as were the Town Steps. ▼

The holiday home of the Crespigny family, built c1775. It was a wealthy and ancient family *'which distinguished itself for beauty, wit and gambling'* but by 1818 the family fortunes had taken a down-turn and for years their big house lay empty and half *'ruinated'*. There was, of course, said to be a ghost. During the next century and a half, the house passed through a number of hands, became a school and then an old peoples' home, until in 1989 it was converted into private dwelling units.

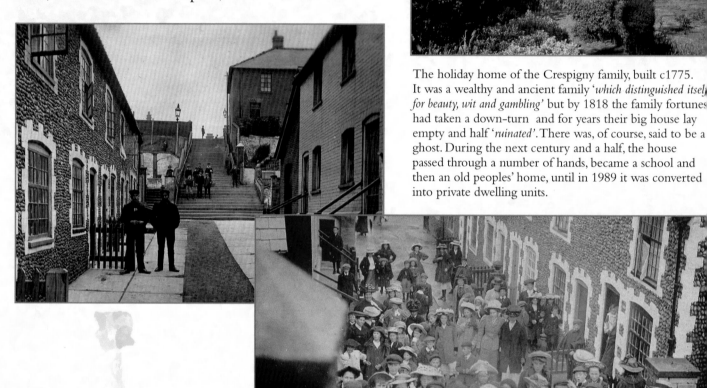

► Whose great grandparents are these?

Between 1826–46 Aldeburgh Meare was drained by the Black Windmill situated near Sluice Cottage between Aldeburgh and Thorpe.

THE GARRETT FAMILY

Newson Garrett, grandson of the founder of the prosperous agricultural machinery works at Leiston, settled his young family at The Uplands in 1840 and soon became the leading business man in the district.

In 1852 he built Alde House complete with ice-house, laundry and Turkish bath.

Newson and Louisa Garrett in old age.

ELIZABETH AND MILLICENT

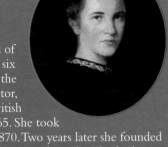

Elizabeth Garrett Anderson, the second of Newson and Louisa's six daughters, fought for the right to train as a doctor, becoming the first British woman doctor in 1865. She took her MD in Paris in 1870. Two years later she founded the new Hospital for Women (later the Elizabeth Garrett Anderson Hospital – she refused to allow it to be called that in her lifetime).

Both Elizabeth and her younger sister Millicent, who married the blind MP Henry Fawcett, were ardent supporters of women's rights. Millicent campaigned tirelessly for over 50 years until her death aged 82.

In 1908, following the death of her husband, Elizabeth, now 71, was elected mayor of Aldeburgh: the first woman mayor in the country.

Elizabeth greeting a young visitor to the Moot Hall.

ALDEBURGH LIFEBOATS

The coast off Aldeburgh is treacherous: the many shoals and sandbanks, often swept by fierce gales, present a real danger to shipping. And during the nineteenth and early twentieth centuries it was a busy seaway.

Life for the early lifeboat-men was harsh and dangerous. A fierce gale in 1855 wrecked or drove ashore seven vessels on the shoals. Newson Garrett was involved in this rescue and 35-year-old Thomas, the father of James Cable, was killed rescuing Newson when he became exhausted.

By 1890 the boat-house at Slaughden had to be abandoned due to erosion and thereafter the lifeboat was kept on the beach $^3/_4$ mile to the north.

In 1825 the newly founded RNLI stationed a lifeboat at Sizewell, crewed mostly by Aldeburgh men. After twenty-six years the station was moved to Slaughden Quay, operating with a new self-righting boat with twelve oars named *Pasco*.

The Aldeburgh Lifeboat memorial in the churchyard.

▲ Anxiously awaiting the *City of Winchester*.

The *Aldeburgh* being launched with the aid of long poles and brute strength. She was said to be unsinkable but after 9 years of service she capsized during a rescue, trapping 6 of her crew underneath. Frantic efforts were made, both to hack through the hull and to lift the boat, but all in vain. The *Aldeburgh* saved at least 152 lives.

James Cable, who retired in 1917 after 50 years service, nearly 30 of them as coxswain. He was awarded many medals and commendations and a lifeboat was named after him.

Edward Z Dresden.

The *James Cable.*

In 1940 the *Abdy Beauclerk*, together with *Lucy Lavers*, the Number 2 lifeboat, were sent to Dunkirk to aid the evacuation of the British Expeditionary Force.

Preparing to launch Abdy B for an exercise. Pulling her on to launching platform.

TODAY'S LIFEBOATS

Today's lifeboat is the *Freddie Cooper,* photographed here by Tony Pick. She is launched by tractor and supported by an Inshore Lifeboat

For the first time since 1870 the Aldeburgh lifeboat has the shelter of her own *Penza* boathouse.

Photos courtesy of Tony Pick. www.coastalimages.co.uk

1907–2007: A CENTURY OF NATURAL DISASTERS

Throughout its history Aldeburgh has fought a desperate battle against the destructive powers of the North Sea. In 1286 there is a record of '*severe inundation in East Anglia*', and thereafter we hear of floods, storms and high tides with horrible regularity.

1953

OUR PICTORIAL RECORD BEGINS IN 1907

In this year The Three Mariners at Slaughden almost surrounded by water.

1907

This was the big one. About 2,000 lives were lost, most of them in the Netherlands. The figures for the United Kingdom were 307 drowned and 32,000 temporarily homeless. In Eastern England roughly 780km² of land was flooded. In Aldeburgh the high tide flooded the town at midnight on January 31. Two hours later the surge came up the river bursting the river wall in two places, flooding the lower end of town for the second time.

Crag Path regularly took a battering. Photographs from 1938 and 1947 show the carnage left behind by the receding water.

1938

1953

1947

1949

Crag Path pounded by waves. Many of the houses in town were damp with salt water for years after the flood.

1953

Fort Green and Mill House in 1949. The seas washed right over the green at the height of the tide on this and several other occasions. The anti-tank blocks were left over from WW2.

Troops filling one of the breaches in the river wall after the flood. During this work a local man was drowned. Billy Burrell received the BEM for rescuing two soldiers who had been swept through the breach.

1953

Rowing up the High Street was the easiest option.

1953

The sea surges through Hertford Place pinning local residents back into odd corners.

1978

9 November 2007: weather forecasts predicted a very high tide and a surge. Sand bags were brought out, the High Street evacuated, but fortunately the surge was not as lethal as predicted and although water flooded over the river wall in two places, there was no breach and only the low-lying areas of Slaughden suffered. ▶

1987

Hurricanes in 1978 and 1987 resulted in damage to property both on land and sea.

1991

A £4.9 million scheme by the Anglian region of the National Rivers Authority provided new and improved defences giving Aldeburgh much greater protection from the sea. But the town is still very vulnerable.

2007

We breathe again! **But what next?**

THE ALDEBURGH BRANCH

For just over a hundred years Aldeburgh was the terminus of an 8-mile single-line branch railway from Saxmundham on the East Suffolk line. The section from Saxmundham to Leiston was opened in 1859, largely to serve Garrett's Engineering Works; after pressure from the inhabitants it was extended to Aldeburgh in 1860.

An elegant carriage meets the train c1865.

EAST SUFFOLK HOTEL, Aldeburgh-on-Sea.   Livery and Bait Stables.   Motor Garage.
CARS & CARRIAGES FOR HIRE.   TELEPHONE NO. 9.   CHARLES A. WARD, PROPRIETOR.

◀ Before the coming of the railway this hostelry was called the *New Inn and Commercial Hotel*. A coach left here every morning at 8 o'clock to meet travellers on the London to Great Yarmouth coach at Saxmundham. When the railway arrived the inn changed its name to the *East Suffolk Hotel*, and the coach service ceased.

An advertising card shows the East Suffolk Hotel c1910. 'Busman' Bill Ward drove a horse-drawn bus from the railway station to the various hotels in the town. Note the phone number: a single digit.

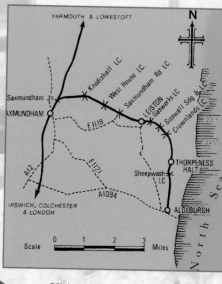

Visitors could now travel in comfort to the fast-developing seaside resort and fish was speedily carried to the hungry markets in London.

Billy Botterill (second from right) ▶ worked at the station for 45 years. He remembered filling large tin cans with boiling water to warm the feet of chilly passengers. When he started work the return fare to London was 6s 6d. (Less than 35p.)

The station gardens won many ▶ awards and were lovingly tended by Billy from 1922 until closure.

The local train from Saxmundham arriving at Aldeburgh Station in 1953. Between 1906 and 1939 the Aldeburgh branch enjoyed the luxury of through coaches to and from Liverpool Street.

A Great Eastern steam train on the Aldeburgh branch line c1960. The last train ran on the 10 September 1966. The station buildings were demolished in 1975 and the site cleared for housing.

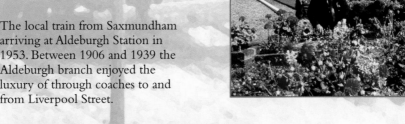

R.I.P.
HERE LIES THE REMAINS
OF
THE ALDEBURGH BRANCH
LINE
1860
SEPTEMBER 1966

PASTIMES

Aldborough Described by Rev. J. Ford was Aldeburgh's first guide book, published in 1819. It reports: *'Such vast improvements to roads and houses in the past 16 years none would believe, helped by great luxury of superb water supply from the Hill. Vice has not yet erected her standard here, the society of Aldeburgh gay without profligacy, pleasurable without debauchery'*.

Cricket match at *The Grammar School*, Crespigny House. 1864.

1884 – James Skelton Anderson, husband of Elizabeth Garrett Anderson, inaugurated the Golf Club and was its first Captain. *'The golf course brought prosperity to the town, but emptied the church pews – they played the game in scarlet coats, deer stalker hats and absurd nether garments'*. From *Sophia's Son* by Dorothy Thompson.

GETTING ABOUT AT THE END OF THE 19TH CENTURY

Fancy dress dance at the Jubilee Hall with *A. Clarke's band*, 1920.

Carnival 1930.

A scene from the promenade sketched in 1863.

The original thatched Golf House c1905. It was devastated by fire in 1910. Note the unmade road; a mere sandy track.

Whist drive 1908; venue unknown.

'Greasy Pole' competition at an early Waterman's Regatta. Aldeburgh Yacht Club.

Aldeburgh Golf Club Lady Members c1911.

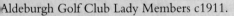

1997 – Centenary Sail Past of the Aldeburgh Yacht Club.

Aldeburgh Town FC c1929.

BENJAMIN BRITTEN AND PETER PEARS BRING MUSIC TO ALDEBURGH

Noye's Fludde was performed in Orford Church in 1958 during the fourteenth Aldeburgh Festival.

Two pictures of Benjamin Britten in relaxed mood.

Costume sketch for *Peter Grimes*.

THEN AND NOW

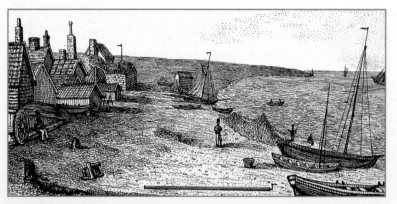

◄ A rather imaginative engraving of 1859 depicts a cluttered Aldeburgh beach looking towards Thorpeness.

Maggie Hamblin's *Scallop* ► was unveiled on the shingle beyond the houses in 2003. A tribute to Benjamin Britten, it bears the legend '*I hear those voices that will not be drowned*'.

Thorpe Haven, at the mouth of the River Hundred, was Aldeburgh's port until it silted up in the 17th century. Originally a footpath led from Aldeburgh to Thorpe over a 'Shatterbone' Bridge, which was replaced in 1889 by the much more substantial Jubilee Bridge. This was dismantled in 1934 when the marshes were drained.

An artist's ► impression of the Shatterbone Bridge.

Station Road, now Victoria Road, leading out of Aldeburgh. On the left is Flintham & Halls 'Albert' Brewery. In the centre is the Station Mill with the station beyond. The Mill was pulled down in 1924. Today the entrance to the Doctors' surgery is on the right beyond the crossing and Church Farm estate is just behind the trees. ▼

▲ Thorpe Bridge and Haven House c1910.

The men who made the Aldeburgh to Thorpeness road. c1866.

The reputed birthplace of the poet George Crabbe, much loved by the Victorians, stood among a huddle of houses between the Moot Hall and the sea. Like all its neighbours, it was washed away by stormy seas towards the end of the 18th century.

A pencil sketch shows the land remaining between the Moot Hall and the sea in 1835. Incidentally, notice the stubby Moot Hall chimneys in this sketch; they were 'improved' by the architect R M Phipson who built on copies of the kitchen chimneys at Hampton Court when he restored the building in 1855.

Promenaders in the 19th century did not need to keep a look-out for cars and nothing hindered them from walking straight on to the beach.

1867

2006

The Brudenell Hotel depicted at two very different times. ▶

WORLD WAR II

Looking from the Martello Tower towards Aldeburgh today the scene is one of pleasant recreation; 1942 presented a very different picture – the coast prepared against invasion.

SLAUGHDEN

Slaughden is the name of the narrow strip of land stretching South of Aldeburgh towards the Martello Tower and Orford Ness. Today there is room only for two sailing clubs and a boat-building yard but once, before erosion took its toll and the river mouth shifted down to Hollesley, it was a thriving commercial centre.

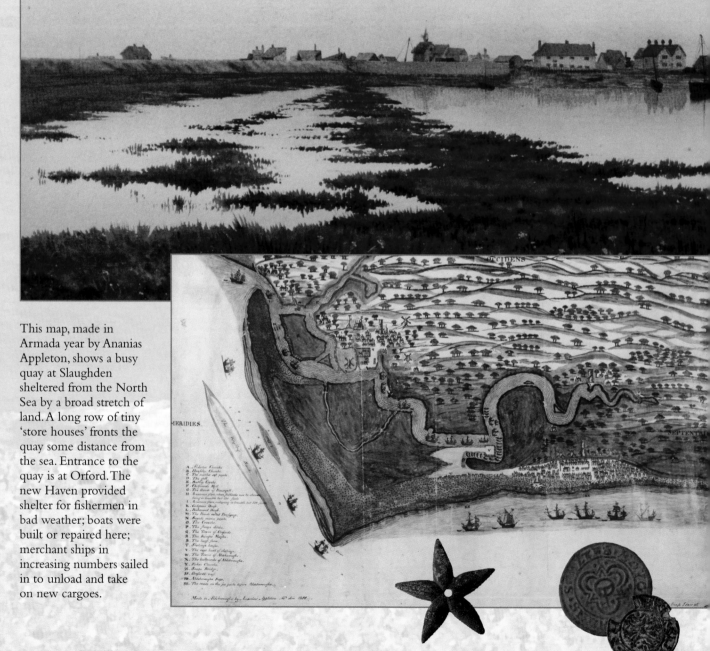

This map, made in Armada year by Ananias Appleton, shows a busy quay at Slaughden sheltered from the North Sea by a broad stretch of land. A long row of tiny 'store houses' fronts the quay some distance from the sea. Entrance to the quay is at Orford. The new Haven provided shelter for fishermen in bad weather; boats were built or repaired here; merchant ships in increasing numbers sailed in to unload and take on new cargoes.

At its peak during the 17th century Slaughden was a very busy place with a *'commodious quay'*, warehouses, and facilities for drying fish and redding (smoking) sprats. Boats bearing coal from Newcastle would call in here and lime, bricks, grain, dairy produce and salt would leave for London and the South. In spring the North Sea fishing fleet would embark on the hazardous voyage to the Faroes and Iceland in search of cod and other deep-sea fish. Some merchants and boat-owners grew rich, but many Aldeburgh sailors lost their lives to stormy seas. Pirate attacks and foreign wars were an additional hazard.

ngraving of Slaughden
uay in 1834.

Looking north towards Aldeburgh.

In 1588 it is recorded that among the *'voluntary ships that came into the fleet after the coming of the Spanish forces upon our coast'* there were three from *Aldborough*: the *Greyhound* with a crew of 40, plus *Jonas* and *Fortune*, each with a crew of 25. These three were part of the Armada campaign but were very small fry, all less than 100 tons.

SLAUGHDEN

In the early 19th century Slaughden was still a busy place, although the biggest boats could no longer be accommodated. There were 2 slaughter-houses; Ramsbottom's coal store; Almond sail loft and fishing tackle shop; and Hunt's shipbuilding yard.

At the heart of the community was the Three Mariners Inn which catered for both the local fisherman and holidaymakers from Aldeburgh.

A peaceful scene c1880.

Slaughden ferry rowed from the west bank of the river to Slaughden Quay. The bell summoned the boatman from the Quay to ferry passengers across from walks along the river bank. The ferry ceased to function in this way c1930, but boatmen still put people across until about 1948. Now the ferry is running again, sponsored by the Alde and Ore Association.

50ft fishing smacks were built here for the Iceland trade. A well in the bottom of the boat was filled with sea water and fish were kept alive until they returned to Slaughden. Once home the fish were clubbed and sold; both men and boats became known as *Codbangers*.

SLAUGHDEN

1892 White's Directory recorded: '*There is a quay at Slaughden; vessels as large as 200 tons receive and discharge cargoes – ship-building yard. About 160 fishing boats – soles, lobsters, herrings, sprats etc. About 20 coasting vessels – average 60-100 tons*'.

The Model Yacht Pond c1900. It was presented to the people of Aldeburgh by Dr Elizabeth Garrett Anderson.

Loading sugar beet on to a sailing barge in 1910 en route for Holland. At this time the roots were very small but provided a great deal of employment to Suffolk villages.

By the end of the 19th century it was clear that Slaughden could not survive. Properties were regularly flooded and people began to move away. This photo, taken in 1910, shows a row of buildings (The Three Mariners on the right) perilously close to the sea. The pub was demolished c1922.

IONIA

She was one of six redundant cod smacks brought to Slaughden in the 1890s by some local fishermen who hoped to make money from the scrap. Ionia was converted into a houseboat and used for holidays. She became a well-known landmark at Slaughden for many years and featured in Kathleen Hale's story of *Orlando (The Marmalade Cat): A Seaside Holiday*. The boat became derelict and a danger to the public and was ceremonially burnt in 1972.

All iced up; Slaughden and the Yacht Club. Winter 1947.

Three pictures chart the end of a house.

35

THE OLD TOWN

In 1894 the High Street was little more than a sandy track well scattered with horse droppings. The only street lighting came from the shops.

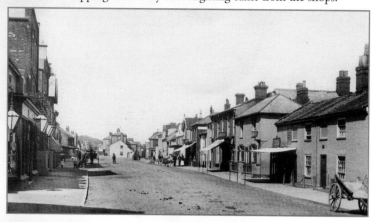

The Old Custom House, listed as 1703, has a fascinating raised front door but no-one is able to explain why. The two big ground-floor windows seem out of scale and were a late addition. Adjoining it to the south are Rosemary Cottage and Lavender Cottage, built c1600 and originally one dwelling: a traditional Suffolk timber-framed house. It is one of the oldest buildings in Aldeburgh although the Cross Keys Inn may pre-date it.

Aldeburgh had its own brewery by 1883: The Albert Brewery. This had developed by 1892 into *Flintham Hall & Co Ltd. brewers, wine and spirit merchants, corn millers and merchants etc* with premises in Station Road (Victoria Road). Flintham's Ales were sold in a number of local hostelries including The Cross Hotel at the bottom of Church Hill.

EDWARD BUTCHER

South End Stores started life in the middle of a row of cottages but around the year 1895 most of the row was demolished to make way for a fine, modern building.

Edward Butcher expanded again c1920. Owen and Clifford Butcher seem to have divided the business: Owen in charge of provisions; Clifford the outfitter. That shop has gone now but the old roof-line can still be recognised above three modern town houses (numbers 245-7).

William Reading claims to have been established as a baker for 100 years. But where were these cottages? There was another Reading bakery in the High Street too, but its whereabouts is not clear. It is on record though that he made the most *'delicious, shiny, sugared, round-top buns with currants in'* which came straight out of the oven for bathers.

The telegraph poles have gone now, otherwise the High Street here looks little changed. Readings' sign may still be faintly seen on the side of the tall building on the left. In 1919, William Hill saw a gap in the market, demolished his outfitters shop, and built the Aldeburgh Cinema (on the right).

A haircut and a newspaper? Three down from the East Suffolk Hotel. Nothing much has changed here.

The old Post Office (where the Sue Ryder Charity Shop and the Ipswich Building Society are now), was destroyed by bombs on 15 December 1942. Within an hour a basic post office service was operating from temporary accommodation although the town itself was cut off from the outside world for a time.

The ladies of Miss Dovey Pettit's *Mill Hand Laundry* at Fort Green. Miss Pettit defended her washing lines against marauding boys for more than 40 years, until, on the 14 February 1938, the laundry was washed away in a storm. It was never rebuilt. Miss Pettit was a remarkable woman; in 1899 she started the District Nursing Service in Aldeburgh; she was one of the founders of the Cottage Hospital; and was mayor of Aldeburgh in 1928. She died aged 86 in 1957.

THE OLD TOWN

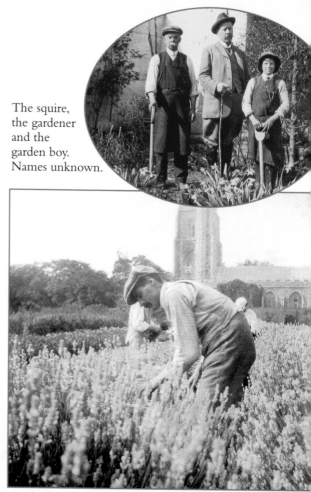

The squire,
the gardener
and the
garden boy.
Names unknown.

The brothers Bert and Ernie Aldridge were both butchers c1935. This was Ernie's shop at Number 157. Imagine the smell on a hot summer's day – and the flies!

Lavender fields opposite the Church.

Watson's Marine Telegraph Signal Station on the Terrace notified Lloyd's of London of the passing of all identifiable ships. It later transferred to Oakley Square and then to the Martello Tower.

'An enchanting toy shop' c1907. Mr and Mrs Smith's toy and fancy goods shop 170-172 High Street.

At Number 62, now Warwick Court, the Aldeburgh Hospital was founded in 1921 with a cottage opposite to serve as an annex. The cost of the two properties was £1,600. The hospital was bombed out in December 1942 but within 36 hours casualties were being treated in an empty house in Park Road which has remained the Cottage Hospital to this day.

In the early days of the 19th century the Shipping Lane passed close to Aldeburgh and rival beach companies built the North and South Lookout Towers to keep watch for vessels signalling for a pilot or to drop/pick up mail. Known as the *Up-towners* and the *Down-towers* they competed with each other for business. Their role was over by the end of the century as coastal trade was lost to the railway.

The men of the Aldeburgh Fire Brigade, formed in 1894. They were equipped with a hand pump drawn by horses which were kept in the stables of the East Suffolk Hotel.

There have been a number of schools in Aldeburgh through the years but the Aldeburgh National School, now the County Primary, is the only one to have stood the test of time. Established in Park Road in1875, it still occupies its original building and is flourishing.

W. Hill was involved in a number of enterprises. Hill & Reading's grocery store opened at Number 64, (Isca House today), possibly as early as 1909.

THE OLD TOWN

HIGH STREET, ALDEBURGH.

The bottom of the High Street, when children could 'play out' alone.

The young ladies of Belstead School enjoy a fire practice. Founded c1906, the school was evacuated in 1939 and failed to return to Aldeburgh.

Between the wars the High Street is still very free of traffic…

…But by 1960 things are changing. There is even a bus.

The local bus service. Hats will be worn!

ALDEBURGH AND THORPENESS

An Aldeburgh interior. Edward Clodd's study displays a photo of him (on the left), enjoying the beach beside Thomas Hardy in August 1909. Clodd was a banker, writer and leading free-thinker. He divided his time between London and Aldeburgh, living in Strafford House on Crag Path between 1889–1930 to which he invited many leading literary figures of the time. ▼

Rev. W. Black converted the old tower mill on Fort Green into a dwelling when its working life was over (1902). His wife (a Dane) was responsible for the Danish inscription over the porch which means: *'The Lord shall preserve thy going out and thy coming in'*. The two cottages were added later. The tower was used as a battery observation post by Coastal Artillery during World War two; a little further north, there were two six inch guns.

O. & C. BUTCHER

James Fisher was established at 131 High Street in 1912; boots and shoes at 5/6d and 6/3d the pair (that's 28p and 31p today).

By 1930 O. & C. Butcher was here.

And before long the size of the shop front had doubled.

41

'ALDBOROUGH...THAT FASHIONABLE AND MUCH-FREQUENTED WATERING-PLACE'

In the opening years of the 19th century visitors began to come to Aldeburgh to enjoy its *'clear and healthy'* air and to sample *'the excellence of its water'*. The Guide Book assures its readers that Aldeburgh *'...is reckoned by physicians to be one of the most healthy places along the eastern shore, and as remarkable for repeated instances of longevity'*. As well as grand hotels, there were some fifteen lodging houses in 1820 not to mention about fifty houses which were *'wholly or in part appropriated for the accommodation of strangers'* and *'charging generally seven shillings per week for each room'*.

The first guide book of Aldeburgh (1819) opens: *'The prevailing taste of the day is to visit a Watering Place....Here the youth of both sexes exhibit their charms; the result is, some may catch a fortune, and some spend one. Some go for amusement, and some for gambling. The doctor sends his patients to the waters to prevent the disgrace of killing them. But the two leading motives are PLEASURE and HEALTH.'*

A young lady paints the view from her bedroom at the end of October 1863. Those red turrets are the northern end of the White Lion Hotel.

In 1860 the White Lion was the principal hotel and one of the oldest. In this print it extends much too far north of the Moot Hall but it can clearly be seen that there is no building beyond it.

By 1869 Wentworth Terrace and North Lodge have joined the White Lion ▶

◀ North Lodge was converted into the Wentworth Castle Hotel which opened in 1900 and was soon attracting many fashionable visitors.

The approach to Aldeburgh c1820, leading to that first eagerly-awaited glimpse of the sea. Fashionable visitors came to bathe, to meet with friends in the library and assembly rooms and, most important of all, to promenade beside the sea in their finest clothes.

The sea-front in 1866. Sun-bathing had not been invented and sea-bathing was a very modest affair indulged in from the shelter of a bathing machine. Aldeburgh bathing machines were lowered into the sea by means of a windlass (much superior to the horses employed by other resorts) and had '*careful and attentive guides*' to assist the timid bather. Machines used by ladies were equipped with a 'cradle' which '*enables the fair bather to plunge into the ocean, without risk, fear, or danger*'. For those unwilling to face the perils of the deep there were '*neat and convenient*' indoor (sea-water) baths, both warm and cold.

Many writers testify to the numbers of small boats sailing or rowing just off the beach at this time and the Guide Book promises the sight of numerous trading vessels and even naval ships approaching very near the shore.

The Esplanade (very close to the sea) at the southern End of town.

This very early photograph is dated c1890. It looks fairly cold and blustery but there are many warmly dressed people walking or sitting on the beach and even a few hardy paddlers. Notice the round bathing hut, a rather unusual design.

'ALDBOROUGH...THAT FASHIONABLE AND MUCH-FREQUENTED WATERING-PLACE'

These two are both called *Eastern Villas* and were engraved in 1868: there the similarity ends.

A delightful, if somewhat imaginative engraving of the view from the Terrace. All prints need to be treated with suspicion when viewed as historical documents, but the Terrace was a fashionable promenade before buildings spoilt the view.

A lively engraving depicts the landward end of a pier opposite the Moot Hall and a fuzzy photograph proves it was there – but only part of it. The Prospectus indicates that it was '*proposed to erect the pier…which will be about 180 yards long, having a minimum depth of water at the outer extremity at the lowest spring tides of 14 1/2 feet*'. Building started in 1876 and four spans were built when a sailing barge ran into it in bad weather, damaging it beyond repair. The rusting ruin remained until 1908 when Elizabeth Garrett Anderson, as Mayor, insisted that it be demolished.

A PAIR OF VERY PRETTY SECOND HOMES!

West Front of Little Casino Aldborough.

▲ The Little Casino, here showing its west front and its view over the sea belonged to *'the Most Noble the Marquis of Salisbury, a nobleman to whom Aldborough is greatly indebted, both on account of his munificent liberality, as well as of his affable demeanour and conciliating manners, which have rendered the place highly gratifying to those, who have been attracted thither by his illustrious name'*. (The name was changed to *Cassino* at some point, Casino being thought to sound too dissipated.)

View from Little Cassino, Aldborough.

The *Marine Villa* of Leveson Vernon, the Lord of the Manor, was much admired, especially for its beautiful gardens and its octagon room ▼ which had wonderful views over the sea.

'ALDBOROUGH...THAT FASHIONABLE AND MUCH-FREQUENTED WATERING-PLACE'

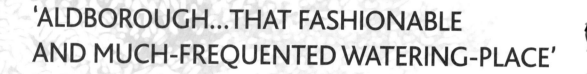

PHOTOGRAPHS DO TELL THE TRUTH

These four show what the young holiday-maker was wearing c1900.

There were still plenty of small craft in evidence and sun-worshipping had arrived.

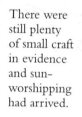

Hardy swimmers could strike out for one of two rafts moored off the beach and patrolled by local fishermen in rowing boats.

PLACES OF LOCAL INTEREST

As travel became easier, the Guide Books began to recommend modest expeditions to places of local interest. Picturesque engravings could be purchased as mementos of these visits:

1. Orford from the Harbour c1820
2. Leiston Abbey 1855
3. Iken Church across the river

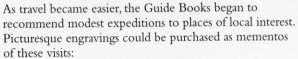

By the end of the 19th century bathing huts were used merely as convenient changing rooms, and soon disappeared altogether.

Not long after the end of WW2 there are groynes on the beach: an attempt to combat erosion. ▶

CHRONOLOGY

Before 500AD	A possible Roman port at the river mouth.
After 500AD	Anglo-Saxon trading post.
1086	Domesday Survey. Roger Malet held the manor of Aldeburgh.
c1490	Aldeburgh emerging as a port.
c1525	Work begins to rebuild and enlarge the present parish church of St. Peter and St. Paul.
1529	First Charter granted by Henry VIII. Town granted a Wednesday market.
c1550	The Moot Hall built. Aldeburgh created a Borough.
1568	Saturday market granted.
1569	Martin Frobisher arrested in Aldeburgh for piracy.
1571	Aldeburgh returns two MPs to Parliament.
1588	The Armada – Three Aldeburgh ships were among the fleet.
Early years of 17th century	Many years of storm and sickness.
1643	William Dowsing visited the church; much destruction resulted.
1646	Seven 'witches' hanged in the town. The river Alde getting shallow.
1672	Battle of Sole Bay. Many sick and wounded sailors cast ashore.
By end 17th century	Decline of trade and shipbuilding – much poverty. Decline in fishing. Empty houses.
Early 19th century	French invasion fears – Martello Tower built. Noble visitors start to arrive. The town begins to expand and become prosperous.
1832	Borough disenfranchised under the Reform Act. Lost its MPs.
1841	Newson Garrett came. Daughter Elizabeth to become first woman doctor.
1851	Lifeboat station at Slaughden. Later lifeboat moves north on to the beach.
1860	Coming of the railway – brings in the visitors.
1899	Lifeboat *Aldeburgh* capsized – six of crew drowned.
1910	The carnival began.
1942	Aldeburgh bombed.
1953	East coast floods brought devastation to the town.
1962	Benjamin Britten made freeman of Aldeburgh.
1966	The last train ran into Aldeburgh station.
2004	The *Scallop* arrives on Aldeburgh beach.